PUFFIN BOO

THE PUFFIN BOOK OF PRAYERS

Dear God,

I'm sorry but I don't feel like praying today. I just can't be bothered. But I do want to be happy today. I want things to go well.

There are times when praying comes easily, and other times when it's hard to think of just the right words. In this varied collection of prayers there is something to suit every mood.

Perhaps you are feeling lonely, facing a dreaded exam, or are experiencing for the first time the death of someone close to you. Or perhaps you are feeling excited about going on a journey, grateful for some particular act of friendship, or just plain glad to be alive. We are daily affected by so many emotions, so many events – and this anthology seeks to reflect this infinite variety. Here are prayers from different countries and different faiths, some of the best-loved traditional prayers, as well as contemporary ones written by children.

The Puffin Book of Prayers will be a source of inspiration and comfort, a book to be enjoyed for years to come.

THE PUFFIN BOOK OF
PRAYERS

Compiled by Louise Carpenter

Illustrated by Shirley Tourret

PUFFIN BOOKS
in association with
Blackie and Son Limited

PUFFIN BOOKS
Published by the Penguin Group
27 Wrights Lane, London W8 5TZ, England
Viking Penguin Inc., 40 West 23rd Street, New York, New York 10010, USA
Penguin Books Australia Ltd, Ringwood, Victoria, Australia
Penguin Books Canada Ltd, 2801 John Street, Markham, Ontario, Canada L3R 1B4
Penguin Books (NZ) Ltd, 182–190 Wairau Road, Auckland 10, New Zealand

Penguin Books Ltd, Registered Offices: Harmondsworth, Middlesex, England

First published as *The Children's Book of Prayers* by Blackie and Son Ltd 1988
Published in Puffin Books 1990
1 3 5 7 9 10 8 6 4 2

Text copyright © Blackie and Son Ltd, 1988
Illustrations copyright © Shirley Tourret, 1988
All rights reserved

The Acknowledgements on page 80 constitute an extension of this copyright page.

Printed by in England by Clays Ltd, St Ives plc

Except in the United States of America,
this book is sold subject to the condition
that it shall not, by way of trade or otherwise,
be lent, re-sold, hired out, or otherwise circulated
without the publisher's prior consent in any form of
binding or cover other than that in which it is
published and without a similar condition
including this condition being imposed
on the subsequent purchaser

CONTENTS

Homes and Families	8
Friends and Fellowship	11
The Almighty Has Done Great Things For Me	13
The Lord is Compassion and Love	16
I'm Sorry, Lord	18
O Lord, You are Good and Forgiving	20
Let Us Remember Others	22
Give Us This Day Our Daily Bread	23
What a Wonderful World!	26
All Creatures Great and Small	30
Where There is Hatred, Let Me Sow Love	33

Blessed are the Peacemakers	36
Welcome to Another Day!	39
Schooldays	45
Special Occasions	48
Journeying On	53
When Times are Hard	55
At the Time of Death	60
You Care For the Sick and Suffering, Lord	63
O Praise Ye the Lord!	66
May the Lord Bless Us	68
Thoughts and Feelings	74

'My way of praying is just praying with an open heart to Him and I get the open answer back.'

Garvan Byrne (11 years old)
Staying at the Helen House
Hospice for children in Oxford

HOMES AND FAMILIES

Mum and Dad

Thank you for my parents, Lord.
I know I don't always agree with them,
And sometimes they don't seem to understand
the way I feel:
But I know they love me,
And want to trust me;
I want to love and trust them too.

Please help me
   to see their point of view—especially when it
   is very different from mine;
   to consider their advice—and even to ask for
   for it;
   to do what they ask me to do—willingly;
   to tell them what I am doing or where I am
   going—at least sometimes.

I want to stand on my own feet, but not
be too independent;
Help me not to shut them out of my life as I
grow older.

I'm glad I have a home—
Show me how to make it a happy one,
Not just for myself but for all of us,
And all who visit us.

Dear Father-and-Mother God,
Thank you for my mother and father
and for all their love to me.
My mum is so loving and my dad so strong
I feel safe with them.
I want all children in the World
to have a happy home like mine.
It makes me sad to know
that many do not have enough to eat
and don't have kind doctors and nurses
to make them well when they are ill.
Thank you for sending Jesus
to tell us about your loving care
for your big family.
Dear God
I love you very much.

George Appleton

A Thanksgiving for a New Sister or Brother

O Lord Jesus, we are very happy today, because a new little baby has come to our home. Thank you for this beautiful gift. Let him/her be a happy and strong baby, and grow up to love you very much: and please help us all to be good to him/her and make a lovely home for him/her.

Dear God, who I feel is like my Father and my Mother, I love my home and am lucky to be in one. So my prayer today is for all those children who haven't one. Dear God, it seems to me that you yourself are a 'home', so will you please come as near as you can to such homeless children? And so, dear God, they can, though homeless, be comforted by sights and sounds and feelings of home, and their hearts may come to rest.

Donald Swann

FRIENDS AND FELLOWSHIP

My friends
Are those who listen when I am sad
Laugh with me when I am happy
Are quiet with me when I am tired
And who trust me.
God, protect them and let me
learn to trust them as they
trust me. Teach me to be
as good a friend as they are
to me. And let me learn
to treat you as the best of
my friends, and to trust you.

Julia Neuberger

Lord, we're going down the Market. We look at all the people: thank you for the friends I meet, the dogs and cats, and all the shops I know. Thank you for the friendly man behind the stalls with new shoes, and lines of clothes flapping, and piles of fruit. Thank you for the ice-cream van, and the chips we take home. Help kids in places where there is not enough to eat.

St Saviour's Priory

Dear God,
Thank you for our friends and for the games
and happy times we have together.
Friends are always such fun.
We are so glad to have friends.
   Thank you, God.

Dear Jesus,
when your friends needed you most,
you were there to help them.
Sometimes,
when our friends are in trouble,
we run away,
or laugh,
or pretend not to care.
Help us to be strong,
and friendly always,
as you were.

THE ALMIGHTY HAS DONE GREAT THINGS FOR ME

Thank you, God, that we have come together.
Thank you, God, that we could giggle together.
Thank you, God, that we could eat together.
Thank you, God, that we could see each other.
Thank you, God, that we could pray together.

(Translated from Swedish)
Barn och bön.

Thank you, Lord Jesus,
for all our happiness.
Thank you especially
for the happiness which takes us by surprise.
Above all we ask you
to lead us toward the surprising discovery
that what most pleases you
will bring the greatest joy to us.

Jamie Wallace

Dear God,
Thank you for the world you have given us to enjoy;
for animals, birds and fishes,
trees and flowers;
for water to drink and food to eat.
Thank you for giving us brains to use
and skill to make things.
Thank you for families to live with and
homes for shelter.
Than you for letting us belong to your family.

Thank you, Father God,
That we can make our faces smile!
It is nice to smile and be happy.
Please help us always to be happy.
Please help us always to smile
and so make other people happy.
Thank you for smiles.

Lord, I can run and jump and shout and SING!
I can skip and clap and stamp and SWING!
Than you for making me alive!

St Saviour's Priory

THE LORD IS COMPASSION AND LOVE

It is not far to go
for you are near.
It is not far to go,
for you are here.
And not by travelling, Lord,
men come to you,
but by the way of love,
and we love you.

Amy Carmichael

Lord, I know
that one of the best ways I can show
my love for you is by loving other people.
Sometimes this is easy—
When I'm with people I like—

Please help me when loving is hard
When people are unkind,
When they don't understand,
When I just don't like them.

Teach me to love as you loved
When you were walking about in Palestine—
Teach me to love as you love NOW—
Everyone
Always.

God bless all those that I love;
God bless all those that love me.
God bless all those that love those that I love
And all those that love those that love me.

      Father God,
          You made me,
          You love me,
          You look after me.
      Thank you, God.

I'M SORRY, LORD

I have a lot to be sorry for this evening, God.
I just wouldn't get up so Dad had to get the car out to
take me to school in time.
I know it messed up his morning.
And then I didn't choose that new boy for my team—
He should have had the chance to play and he looked so
miserable.
Teacher read my essay to the Class and said it
was very good: but you know and I know that Mum
thought it out.
I should have told the teacher I wasn't that clever but
I didn't.
I know it says we shall be forgiven if we own up.
I'm really trying to do that now so please don't
change your mind.

Fraser McLuskey

It's difficult to tell anyone else
I feel sorry because then they'll know
what a fool I've been, but I can tell
you. I shouldn't have done it.
It makes me feel awful. You think
I ought to own up?
All right. I will.
Help me. Stay with me. Keep loving me,
and I will.

David Scott

I Wish I Hadn't

Father,
I wish I hadn't behaved like that today.
I didn't really want to
but I couldn't stop myself.

There are two sides to me,
A good side and a bad side, and today
the bad was on top.

Please forgive me
I am truly sorry.

Help me to see my faults
and to overcome them.

Help me, too, not to lash back
when others hurt me.
Teach me to forgive them
and treat them as friends.

O LORD, YOU ARE GOOD AND FORGIVING

Even if I have gone astray, I am thy child, O God; thou art my father and mother.

Arjan
(Died 1616—Sikh)

O God,
We ask you to forgive us
for
    the things we have not thought about
    the jobs we have not done
    the words we have not spoken

We ask you to help us
    to think
    and do
    and say
the right things at the right times.

Forgiving Others

Dear God,
I get angry when other people bully me,
   when they talk about me behind my back,
   and when they gang up against me.
Help me to forgive them.

I want to hit other people
   when they tell lies and shout at me,
   and when they say their parents are rich and clever.
Help me to forgive them.

Your son, Jesus Christ shows us how to forgive;
He forgave those who crucified him.
Help me to stand up for myself without hating others.
Help me to be calm and strong when things get hard.
Help me to be more like Jesus every day.

I ask this in his name.

Alan Webster

Dear Father God,
I am very sorry for everything I have done wrong.
Sometimes I have been lazy and disobedient;
Sometimes I have said 'no' when someone has asked me for help;
Sometimes I have been greedy, selfish or nasty to others.

Please forgive me and help me to do better.
And help me to forgive others when they hurt me;
For the sake of Jesus, my Lord.

LET US REMEMBER OTHERS

Dear God,
I send my love to all children, everywhere,
In the hot countries and the cold countries,
Specially the little ones without enough to eat
And no toys. Take care of all of us and help us
To live happily as brothers and sisters and never
To hurt each other. Teach us to enjoy together this
Lovely world — the trees and the flowers, all the
Animals, our families and friends, our games and
our food.
Please, dear God, send your angels to help us and
Give us your blessing.

Heather McConnell

For the Unhappy

O Jesus, when I am happy and surrounded by love, I want to remember everyone who is unhappy, and to ask your love and pity for them all. Help me not to forget those who are hungry, and without friends, and lonely, and those far away from all they love. Show me how to pray for them, and to make things as happy for them as I can.

For the Lonely

Dear Lord Jesus, please bless those who are lonely.
Bless children who have no friends to play with, and
bless old people who have no one to visit them.
Please let them understand that you are always with
them and always loving them.
Please help me to be kind and friendly to lonely people.

GIVE US THIS DAY OUR DAILY BREAD

Blessed are you, Lord our God, King of the Universe, who feeds the entire world in his goodness—with grace, with kindness and with mercy. He gives food to all life for his kindness is eternal . . . Blessed are you, God, who nourishes all.

Jewish Grace

The bread is pure and fresh,
The water cool and clear
Lord of all life, be with us
Lord of all life, be near.

African Grace

My God, I thank you for my food. It is you that allows the rice, the beans, the wheat, the fruit, the animals and the vegetables to grow. I thank you for the food that is on the table. Thank you very much, Lord.

(Translated from Portuguese)
Elizete Simon, 11 years old,
Independência, Brazil

Bread is a lovely thing to eat—
God bless the barley and the wheat;
A lovely thing to breathe is air—
God bless the sunshine everywhere;
The earth's a lovely place to know—
God bless the folks that come and go!
Alive's a lovely thing to be—
Giver of life—we say—bless thee!

Here a little child I stand,
Heaving up my either hand;
Cold as Paddocks though they be,
Here I lift them up to Thee,
For a Benizon to fall
On our meat, and on us all. *Amen.*

Robert Herrick

What God gives, and what we take,
'Tis a gift for Christ His sake:
Be the meale of Beanes and Pease,
God be thank'd for those, and these.
Have we flesh, or have we fish.
All are Fragments from His dish.

Robert Herrick

WHAT A WONDERFUL WORLD!

To see a World in a Grain of Sand
And a Heaven in a Wild Flower,
Hold Infinity in the palm of your hand
And Eternity in an hour.

William Blake

Amergin

I am the wind which breathes upon the sea,
I am the wave of the ocean,
I am the murmur of the billows,
I am the ox of the seven combats,
I am the vulture upon the rocks,
I am a beam of the sun,
I am the fairest of plants,
I am a wild boar in valour,
I am a salmon in the water,
I am a lake in the plain,
I am a word of science,
I am the point of the lance in battle,
I am the God who creates in the head the fire.
Who is it who throws light into the meeting on the mountain?
Who announces the ages of the moon?
Who teaches the place where couches the sun?

Anon

God our Father,
   You have given us a lovely world.
Thank you for hills and valleys
   trees and flowers
      sunshine and rain
         animals and fish.
Thank you for my mother and father
   brothers and sisters
      relations and friends.
Help me not to damage your world
   but to treat it with care
      and to love all whom I meet.
Above all, teach me to love you, our Father,
   and Jesus Christ whom you have sent.

Donald Coggan

Pippa's Song

The year's at the Spring,
And the day's at the morn;
Morning's at seven;
The hill-side's dew-pearl'd;
The lark's on the wing;
The snail's on the thorn;
God's in his heaven—
All's right with the world!

Robert Browning

God is in the water, God is in the dry land, God is in the heart.
God is in the forest, God is in the mountain, God is in the cave.
God is in the earth, God is in heaven . . .
Thou art in the tree, thou art in its leaves,
Thou art in the earth, thou art in the firmament.

Govind Singh
(Sikh)

ALL CREATURES GREAT AND SMALL

Show love to all creatures, and thou wilt be happy; for when thou lovest all things, thou lovest the Lord, for he is all in all.

*Tulsi Das
(1532–1623—Hindu)*

A Prayer for Little Things

Please God, take care of little things,
The fledglings that have not their wings,
Till they are big enough to fly
And stretch their wings across the sky.
Take care of small new lambs that bleat,
Small foals that totter on their feet,
And all small creatures ever known
Till they are strong to stand alone.

Eleanor Farjeon

The Prayer of the Little Ducks

Dear God,
give us a flood of water.
Let it rain tomorrow and always.
Give us plenty of little slugs
and other luscious things to eat.
Protect all folk who quack
and everyone who knows how to swim.

Carmen Bernos de Gasztold

Prayer for a Sick Animal

Dear Father God,
My pet is sick and I am sad. Please make her better and comfort her if she's in pain. She can't tell me what she's feeling, but help her to know that I care and will look after her and help her all I can, just as I'm looked after when I'm ill. Please bless her and give her the strength she needs to recover.

O Lord Jesus, please make me kind to all animals that I meet, and help everyone else to be good to them too. Help me to learn about all the things that animals do for us, and to try to do things for them, because you were always loving and kind.

Father, we thank you for animals that help us, for cows, sheep, and horses; dogs that guard us, and those that guide the blind. We thank you, too, for all rare and strange animals, and for those that make us laugh. May we take good care of them all.

The Prayer of the Tortoise

A little patience,
O God,
I am coming.
One must take nature as she is!
It was not I who made her!
I do not mean to criticise
this house on my back—
it has its points—
but you must admit, Lord,
it is heavy to carry!
Still,
let us hope that this double enclosure,
my shell and my heart,
will never be quite shut to you.

Carmen Bernos de Gasztold

For Our Pets

God, our Father, Maker of all animals, please help us to realize that you have to put us in charge of our pets and that they depend on us for food and proper care. May we always be loving and gentle with them, not teasing nor cruel. Thank you for the love and friendliness they show us.

Zinnia Bryan

WHERE THERE IS HATRED, LET ME SOW LOVE

Let me see other people, Heavenly Father, as Jesus saw them, not separated from me by colour, or divided by race, but all joined with me as members of your world-wide family. May the golden day come soon when this world-wide family shall be established throughout the world, and we shall all be brothers and sisters with Jesus as our elder brother and our king.

Donald Soper

Dear Lord of Love, help us, who have so much, to share what we have with our poor, who have so little; help us who live in good and happy homes to remember those who have bad ones, or who are strangers in our land; help those of us whose skins are white to love and respect our brothers and sisters, who often suffer so much because theirs are black or brown, for you are the God and Father of us all, and we are all equally your children.

Nadir Dinshaw

Let us hold hands in a circle and remember Jesus.
How he began this world with songs for people everywhere.
Let us stand together, watch where the sun divides—
and stretch our arms out to those that are far away.
If we call, they may hear us, join the friendship we share
between us, and the laughter between brothers and sisters.
Let us think of Jesus and pray for others too
so that there is no one lonely under his skies.
We must watch the light shine on these hills again;
follow the stars, look up to where God's kingdom
etches joy in our hearts until we are in heaven,
where peace and understanding are with us always.
Let us hold hands in a circle and remember Jesus.

Celia Purcell

Dear God,
You have shown us by the loveliness of the rainbow, which so often follows a storm, that the light without which we cannot live and grow is made up by the perfect blending of different colours. Help us to see that the light of your love embraces men and women and girls and boys of different nations, faiths and colours in one great human family. So may we learn to live, work and play together always in and through your love.

William W. Simpson

BLESSED ARE THE PEACEMAKERS

O God, make us children of quietness, and heirs of peace.

St Clement

We thank you Lord for bringing us safely through five thousand years of often troubled history to this day. Shield us from holding the prejudices that others hold against us and help us to bring peace and harmony into this world so that everyone will praise your great name O Lord king of peace. We wait for the day when all people will perform only good deeds and live together in perfect harmony. Only then will we be able to appreciate this beautiful world that you have given us which we have used so badly in the past. But most important; Lord, help us to be at peace with ourselves for, without being at peace with ourselves, how can we be at peace with anyone else? Blessed are you Lord who brings light into darkness and turns hatred into love.

Paul Daniel Conway

I thank you for having freed us from world wars and I ask that you would bring peace to the world because it is so painful to know that there are children in the world that are losing their parents. Illuminate the minds and understanding of those who are to blame for the wars so that they know what they are doing. I ask you because I know you can do everything.

Elsa Gonzalez Lasalle,
Bayamon, Puerto Rico.

Dear Lord,
in your word
you teach us
to love
one another.
We ask you,
dear Jesus,
prevent war
and bloodshed,
prevent us and
all the others
from hunger
and sickness.
Let people
stop killing
each other.
Forgive us
our sins
in your name
alone.

Leonard H. Dengeinge,
*   12 years old,*
* Ongwediva, Namibia.*

Lord, make me an instrument of your peace;
where there is hatred let me sow love,
where there is injury let me sow pardon,
where there is doubt let me sow faith,
where there is despair let me give hope,
where there is darkness let me give light,
where there is sadness let me give joy.

O divine master, grant that I may
not try to be comforted but to comfort,
not try to be understood but to understand,
not try to be loved but to love.

Because it is in giving that we are received,
it is in forgiving that we are forgiven,
and it is in dying that we are born to eternal life.

(Attributed to St Francis of Assisi)

WELCOME TO ANOTHER DAY!

Morning Prayers

Lord, thou knowest how busy I must be today—
if I forget thee do not thou forget me. *Amen.*

Sir Jacob Astley before the Battle of Edgehill

Now another day is breaking,
Sleep was sweet and so is waking.
Dear Lord, I promised you last night
Never again to sulk or fight.
Such vows are easier to keep
When a child is sound asleep.
Today, O Lord, for your dear sake,
I'll try to keep them when I wake.

Ogden Nash

Lord Jesus take my hand
and lead me through this day;
Bless all I meet in home or street
While working or at play.

Lord Jesus take my hand
and let me never stray
far from your side, but be my guide
in all I do or say.

Lord Jesus take my hand
and place it in your own;
Just hold me tight from morn till night
and I'll not be alone.

Sister Mary Raphael

Angel of God, my guardian dear,
To whom God's love commits me here,
Ever this day be at my side
To light, to guard, to rule and guide.
Amen

O Lord God, help me and all other children to remember you today, and always to do the things that you would like us to do. Thank you for taking care of us all through the night. Teach us to show our thanks to you more every day, by being good and happy and unselfish, knowing that you are near us in our work and our play, and that you love us all the time.

Be thou a bright flame before me,
Be thou a guiding star above me,
Be thou a smooth path below me,
Be thou a kindly shepherd behind me,
Today—tonight—and forever.

St Columba of Iona

Evening Prayers

O Lord Jesus Christ, who didst receive the children who came to thee, receive also from me, thy child, this evening prayer. Shelter me under the shadow of thy wings, that in peace I may lie down and sleep; and do thou waken me in due time, that I may glorify thee, for thou alone art righteous and merciful. Amen

Eastern Church

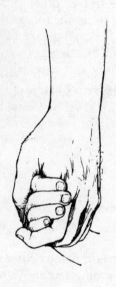

O Lord Jesus, I know that you care for all children, and have watched over me through the day. Bless me tonight as you blessed the little children who were brought to you on earth. Thank you for all the happiness of the day. Help me every day to become more like you. Forgive me for everything wrong that I have done, and help me to want to please you best of all.

> Matthew, Mark, Luke and John,
> Bless the bed that I lie on.
> Four corners to my bed,
> Four Angels there be spread:
> One at the head, one at the feet,
> And two to guard me while I sleep.
> God within, and God without,
> And Jesus Christ all round about;
> If any danger come to me,
> Sweet Jesus Christ deliver me.
> Before I lay me down to sleep
> I give my soul to Christ to keep;
> And I die before I wake,
> I pray that Christ my soul will take.

May the Lord Jesus Christ, who is the splendour of the eternal light, remove from our hearts all darkness, now and for evermore.

Night-time

Dear God, it seems so odd calling you God. It makes you seem so far away. And yet when I look up at all the stars in the night sky, I feel you are out there, looking down on us all. And when I fall asleep the stars go on looking down and I know that you, too, are watching over me. And when I wake up in the morning you will be there with the sun. Perhaps the stars are all your angels watching over us? Perhaps each star is a guardian angel? Perhaps each of us has a star as well as a guardian angel to ourselves? Just as when Jesus was born he had a star to himself. Oh, God, let my star watch over me this night. Goodnight, God.

James Roose-Evans

SCHOOLDAYS

Beginning of Term

God our Father, we ask you to bless our school, our friends,
Our teachers and all the people who look after us here.
Please bless the new children. Show us how to help them and make
Us kind and friendly like Jesus.

Before Going to School

A schoolday begins
and we think of you, God
Lord hear our prayer
> We thank you
> for the brain that can think
> for the memory that remembers
> for the ears, for words and music.
> We thank you
> for the mouth that can speak
> for the hands that work
> for the eyes that see and read.
>> Help us today
>> to understand what we learn.
>> Let the knowledge be put to good use.
>> Let us bring joy ourselves
>> both now and when we are grown-ups.
God our Father
we leave our day
in your hands.

(Translated from Swedish)
Jag vill tala med Gud,
by Margareta Melin

O God we thank you that we can pray to you as our Father and can know, as Jesus taught, that you care for every one of us. We thank you that though there are so many people in the world everyone matters to you and that you have given to each of us different gifts. Help us to understand this as we work with each other in our School and give us generous hearts to enjoy the success of others while doing everything as well as we can ourselves. As we learn more of your world show us if there are ways in which we can make life happier for others of your children and send your spirit of love into our hearts. We ask this in the name of him who came to show the world how much you cared for it, Jesus Christ our Lord.

Diana Reader Harris

Exams

I hate exams;
The questions don't always seem fair
Sometimes they're too hard anyway.
I suppose we've got to have them,
But I wish we didn't:
Teachers always say it will be all right
If we've worked!
I haven't always worked hard, but who does,
Apart from you, Lord?
I don't want special favours,
but help me and my form
To do as well as we can
And certainly as well as we deserve.

Lord, make my heart strong to face all trials, knowing that you love me solely for what I am, and that your love will never fail me. I believe that perfect love casts out fear; help me to feel this in my heart.

Anne Ridler

A Difficult Day

Father let me tell you something:
I hated school today.
My friends were nasty,
my teacher shouted,
and someone tripped me up
in the playground.
Lord God my Father
thank you for listening,
and help me to enjoy tomorrow.
                               Amen

SPECIAL OCCASIONS

Christmas

O God, our loving Father, help us rightly to remember the birth of Jesus, that we may share in the songs of the angels, the gladness of the shepherds, and the worship of the wise men. May the Christmas morning make us happy to be your children, and the Christmas evenings bring us to our beds with grateful thoughts, forgiving and forgiven, for Jesus' sake. Amen

Robert Louis Stevenson

Love came down at Christmas,
Love all lovely, Love Divine;
Love was born at Christmas,
Star and Angels gave the sign.

Worship we the Godhead,
Love Incarnate, Love Divine;
Worship we our Jesus:
But wherewith for sacred sign?

Love shall be our token,
Love be yours and love be mine,
Love to God and all men,
Love for plea and gift and sign.

Christina Rossetti

O Lord Jesus, we remember you as a Holy Baby on this day. We love you for coming to earth and being a child like us. We would like to have knelt at your crib and brought you presents of flowers and toys and beautiful things. Thank you for making your birthday such a happy day for everyone. Help us to love you more and more and try every year to grow more like you.

Easter

O Lord Jesus, I want to be happy today, and to love you more than I have ever done before, because you must have been happy on that Easter Day so many years ago, and must have been so glad to know that your friends would be happy once again. You suffered and died because of your love for us, and now that suffering is over and you are with God in Heaven. Keep us in your care, and make us more like you, so that one day we may be good enough to live with you for ever.

Help me today, Lord Jesus, to remember you with all the love of my heart, because you suffered and died on this day long ago. Teach me to understand that you died for love, that I may grow loving like you, and be afraid of nothing but grieving God.

The Christening of a Baby

O Lord Jesus, our dear little baby is going to be christened to-day. Please receive him/her into your family, as you took the little children up in your arms and blessed them long ago. And please ask your holy angels to watch over him/her always.

The New Year

I want to ask your help, Lord Jesus, in all the coming year. Each year that I live I want to learn to be a little more like you. You have shown me what it is like to be really good, by always being perfectly obedient and loving in the carpenter's shop at Nazareth. It is difficult for me to learn because I am so weak, but please hear my prayer and teach me to be strong.

A Birthday Prayer

It's my birthday today, God. Hurray! I feel happy to be alive and want to thank you for all the lovely things in my life and the world around me. Now I'm a year older, help me to grow bigger in a way that pleases you and help me always to stay close to you.

JOURNEYING ON

Why do I always forget to say my prayers
when I go on a journey? Perhaps
because there's so much else to do.
Could being excited be a prayer?
Could let me enjoying myself be a prayer?
Seeing things through the window;
the drinks at the service station;
my mum and dad happier than usual;
the car songs and the games. My mum
has a good way of not being sick in the car:
you've got to look out of the front window
and not read. I like falling asleep
in the car and waking up a hundred miles
nearer the end; setting off while it's still dark.
The things I've packed specially for me.
The holiday money in my purse.

David Scott

Before a Holiday

Bless me now, Lord Jesus, before I begin the holiday you have given me. Help me to make it a happy day for all I love. I want to thank you for my life and strength and happiness, and to learn to love you more every day. Help me to remember you in all my games and pleasures, that I may do nothing to grieve your love. And please go with me everywhere I go, that I may be safe in your keeping.

For Those who are Going Away from our Home

O Jesus, I want to ask you to watch over those I love who are going away from me. Take care of them on their journey, guard them from harm while they are away, and bring them home again happily and safely.

WHEN TIMES ARE HARD

Feeling Angry

Sometimes I find it hard Lord
to sit still and listen to you.
My anger gets in the way.
and my mind criss-crosses
with nasty thoughts.
Help me to share my anger with you
and not to let it swallow me up.
Help me not to make other people
angry with me,
but show me how to be loving.

Timothy King

Thank you Father
for loving me
even when I am
cross and angry.

Timothy King

Prayer From a Disabled Child

Lord, you were disabled
when you hung on the cross;
yet that is how you showed us
God's love.
May the power of that love
shine through my weakness,
my disability, to show
God's glory to the world.

Susan Mabe

Lord,
I am unhappy—nothing seems to be going right
for me.
If it is my fault
that life is so difficult at the moment,
Please show me where I have gone wrong.

If it is my fault,
Give me courage to accept all my difficulties
And to learn something of value from them.

You seem very far away—
Help me to know for certain that
you are beside me all the time.

Lord, I want to believe in your power to
help me—
Forgive me when I find it hard to do so.

Feeling Frightened

I'm often frightened, Lord.
Not the sort of fright when there's danger
—I usually don't take much notice of that
and even enjoy the thrill.
I'm scared when I know what I ought to do
But don't want to do it.
Being your 'faithful soldier and servant'.
—As the priest says when he baptises
anyone and puts the cross on his forehead—
Isn't always easy.
The fact is, the harder I try
The more difficult it becomes.

Dear God,
I often feel frightened.

>Sometimes big people frighten me.
>Sometimes I cannot do what the teacher wants at school.
>I'm scared when grown-ups quarrel and shout
>>and when they lose their jobs.
>I'm scared when I lie awake in the dark
>>and when I have bad dreams.

When I'm frightened
>It's like a dark cloud shutting out the sunshine.

Help me to be brave.
Help me to trust my friends.
Help me to trust you.
Help me to laugh and have good fun.
Show me how to help others
>When they are frightened and sad.

Alan Webster

Lord, I'm scared. You know how that feels. My new school is so big: I don't know any of the teachers and I miss my old friends. Stay with me: help me to smile and then I shall make new friends.

St Saviour's Priory

Feeling Lonely

I feel lonely today. Everyone else seems to have friends, but I don't. Help me to know that you, God, are a friend to everyone and that you are the greatest friend any of us could ever hope for.

Dear God I am upset today,
nothing seems to have gone right.
People seem to hurt me so easily,
and don't seem to realize it.
When I am feeling like this
it's good to know that you care.

Timothy King

Dear Lord Jesus, please help me to keep on trying when things are hard.
You never gave up when you had to carry your cross.
When I have hard work to do, help me to keep on trying.
When it is hard to be good, help me to keep on trying.
When it is difficult to do as I am told, help me to keep on trying.
Dear Lord Jesus, I need your help.
Thank you for showing me how to persevere.

AT THE TIME OF DEATH

Lord Jesus, you taught us to let the little children
   come to you,
and not to try to stop them;
into your loving hands we commend your child
   (my brother/sister)
for he/she is yours in death as in life.
Gather him/her to yourself gently, and in peace;
that he/she may be happy with you, and,
freed from all pain and fear,
may enjoy his/her new life for evermore.

Written for the funeral of Eleanor, aged 6

Heavenly Father, thank you for blessing us with
the precious gift of (Name).
for guiding us in the way we have loved and cared for him/
   her,
and have helped him/her to grow into the world;
and for the great love which we have all shared through
Jesus Christ our Lord.

Charles Taylor

Dear Lord
Thank you for grandparents. My gran was fun. She used to laugh a lot and read me stories. She was warm and friendly. I'll miss her now she's dead. But I know I'm lucky—some kids never even meet their grandparents. It's funny to think that one day I'll be old like my gran. I hope I'll be as smiley and kind as her.
Thank you, Lord, for grandparents.

Dear God:
Please hear my prayer
Give me the strength
To accept your will
And forgive me for
My sins if any.
If you think it fit
To take me
Then please give
Strength and courage
To those who love me
And help me
Not to rail in self-pity.
Asking why?
But to have faith
And to know that . . .
Your will is best
Help me!
Oh, please help me
To trust you
Not from fear but
Because of Love and
Faith.

Gitanjali
*(Written by an Indian girl
shortly before she died.)*

Dear God,
My pet died today. It makes me feel empty. There'll be no one waiting by the door when I get home from school looking pleased to see me, and no one warm and furry to hug when I feel unhappy. Mum says we can get a new one, but it won't be the same. God, I know I've got to accept it, but it's so hard. Thinking of all the good times we had together makes me feel happy and sad at the same time. I know I have a lot to thank you for God, but I can't understand why he had to die. Please help me.

YOU CARE FOR THE SICK AND SUFFERING, LORD

It's not always so bad being ill.
My mum is so kind and brings me comics.
The doctor comes in his doctory clothes
and sits on my bed. I don't have to get up
so early in the morning. I can read my book
and listen to the world through the window.
I think I'll get better.
I'm sure everything will be all right in the end.

David Scott

For All Sufferers

O Lord, I want to ask you to be with everyone who is ill today. I know how kind you were to all people who were suffering, and how you tried to make them better. Show me what I can do to help anyone who is ill or in pain, and make me always brave and cheerful when I am hurt or ill.

Watch thou, dear Lord, with those who wake, or watch, or weep to-night, and give thine angels charge over those who sleep.
Tend thy sick ones, O Lord Christ; rest thy weary ones; bless thy dying ones; soothe thy suffering ones; shield thy joyous ones; and all for thy Love's sake.

St Augustine

I prayed to God; he heard my prayer,
And made a little child his care:
When I was sick he healed my pain,
And gave me health and strength again.
Oh, let me now his grace implore,
And love and praise him evermore!

D. A. Thrupp

Dear Lord
I pray today for all people in hospitals. Comfort them in their suffering and pain and be with them if they're feeling lonely and sad. Please bless all those looking after them: the nurses and doctors, their families and friends and all those who work in the hospitals. I know some people find it difficult coming out of hospital when they haven't got a family to go home to. Please be with them, too, Lord. I ask all this in your name as the great Comforter and Healer of all.

For Disabled Children

When I meet and work with children who are not so well and strong as I am, help me, God, to help them in the right way, so that we can all work together and take our share, for Jesus' sake.

O PRAISE YE THE LORD!

Blessed art Thou, O Lord our God, King of the universe,
who createst thy world every morning afresh.

> All that we see rejoices in the sunshine,
> All that we hear makes merry in the Spring:
> God grant us such a mind to be glad after our kind,
>   And to sing
>   His praises evermore for everything.

Christina Rossetti

MAY THE LORD BLESS US

God's Blessings

Thank you, Father, for the many blessings
You give us so generously. The blessings
we value and see so clearly in our lives,
as well as those of which we are unaware—
or take for granted.
Among the blessings we see are the love and
protection that comes directly from you,
or indirectly, through the loving care of parents,
grandparents, family and friends, as well as
through the guidance of our bible, our teachers,
our religious leaders, and others who give us
the benefit of their knowledge and experience.
And the blessings of which we are unaware—
the effort of our government to keep peace at home
and harmony among the family of nations; and
the dedication of those who care for the folk
who cannot care for themselves.
And the blessings we take for granted—the blessing
of the sunshine and the rain, of friendship, of
comfort when we feel sad, the blessing of freedom
(to do good or bad!).
Above all, the blessing of being able to wake up each day,
strong in body and mind, to praise you, Lord,
for *all* your blessings.

Jeffrey M. Cohen

My good angel
stay with me
today
and don't
let me do
what is wrong.

*Fanny Camara-Macauley
8 years old,
Sierra Leone.*

O heavenly Father, protect and bless all things that have breath: guard them from all evil and let them sleep in peace.

Albert Schweitzer when a child

Open our eyes
for Your truth.

Open our hearts
for Your joy.

Open our eyes
for Your will.

Open our hands
for Your work.

Open our hearts
for Your love.

Open our hands
for one another.

(Translated from Swedish)
Jag vill tala med Gud, by Margareta Melin

O most merciful Redeemer, Friend, and Brother,
May we know thee more clearly,
Love thee more dearly
Follow thee more nearly,
For ever and ever.

St Richard of Chichester—1197–1253

God in all things,
you speak to girls and boys, and men and women,
in every land and all languages,
people of different colours and beliefs.
With wise people in past and present we ask:
Lead us from falsehood to truth,
Lead us from darkness to light,
Lead us from weakness to fullness of life.
Lead us, Lord, in your goodness.
Make your way plain for us wherever we go.

Geoffrey Parrinder

Jesus Christ, Thou child so wise,
Bless mine hands and fill mine eyes,
And bring my soul to Paradise.

Hilaire Belloc

O Lord! I am a child; enable me to grow beneath the shadow of thy loving kindness. I am a tender plant; cause me to be nurtured through the outpourings of the clouds of thy bounty. I am a sapling of the garden of love; make me into a fruitful tree.

Thou art the Mighty and the Powerful, and thou art the All-Loving, the All-Knowing, the All-Seeing.

Abdu'l-Bahá

O God, guide me, protect me, illumine the lamp of my heart and make me a brilliant star. Thou art the Mighty and the Powerful.

Abdu'l-Bahá

Protect me, O Lord;
My boat is so small,
And your sea is so big.

Old Breton Prayer

God be in my head
And in my understanding;
God be in my eyes;
And in my looking;
God be in my mouth,
And in my speaking;
God be in my heart,
And in my thinking;
God be at my end,
And at my departing.

Sarum Missal

THOUGHTS AND FEELINGS

Mountains are very still,
they just sit and sit and sit.
They point to your greatness, O God,
silent and quiet.
Help me to be still and silent,
like a mountain.
Sitting still, listening to your voice.

Timothy King

Dear God
I'm sorry but I don't feel like praying today. I just can't be bothered.
But I do want to be happy today. I want things to go well. And not just for me either—there's my family, of course, and my friends, and if I think about it, I suppose I even want those people I don't like to be all right, too!
And then there are all those in the world I've never met and never think about. So many of them have a horrible life with troubles and sickness and pain. But I'm sure, Lord, that despite all their suffering lots of them make the effort to pray each day. I'm sure too, Lord, that you know them and love them and help them at least as much as you do me. O dear God, help me to be more a part of your whole world.
Help me to care more and to pray more.

John Robson

Faith

Heavenly Father, we thank you that you give your children a faith to live by, which teaches us to treasure the marvels of your world and helps us to find a meaning and purpose for our lives.

Our religion tells us of your mercy and kindness to those who lived hundreds of years ago and shows how that same care has been with people in every generation.

Our faith inspires us too with hope for the future and the will to work for a better world.

As we grow in our faith help us to understand more about the faiths of others—so that   Christians and Jews,
                                    Muslims and Sikhs,
                                    Hindus and Buddhists
May stretch out hands of friendship to each other,
Raise them together in worship of you,
And use them in service of each other and of all who are poor or ill, sad or hungry.

We ask this in your name.

Marcus Braybrooke

God

Eternal Spirit,
you are around us and within us,
every day and in all ways.
We do not need to call you to come here,
as if you were far away,
for you are always near us.
We do not need to tell you what we want,
for you know more about us than we know ourselves.
We do not need to persuade you,
as if you were not willing to help,
for you love us better than we love ourselves.
But because we are weak and do not know our true needs,
so we ask for help and guidance.
We seek, and knock, and ask.
We open our minds to hear your voice.
We give our bodies to follow your way in daily life.

Geoffrey Parrinder

I believe that God is in me as the sun is in the colour and fragrance of a flower—the Light in my darkness, the Voice in my silence.

Helen Keller

There is One and only One God.
He is the Creator of this universe.
He is All-powerful, Omnipresent and Merciful.
We are all his children and he deeply
loves us all irrespective of our race,
colour or creed.
Similarly, he wants us also to love
everyone in the same way.
He helps those who seek his help
through a sincere prayer.
Similarly, he wants us also to help
those who need our help.
This pleases him most and, in return,
being a generous Father, he bestows upon
us all the bounties of life.

Harmindar Singh

God is with me now.
God sees me.
God hears me.
God smiles at me.
God loves me.
God wants me . . .
now and always.

St Saviour's Priory

Acknowledgements

The Publisher would like to thank the following for their kind permission to reprint copyright material in this book:

Khushi Badruddin for the prayer by Gitanjali (p 61) © Khushi Badruddin 1982; The Catholic Truth Society for 'For the Lonely' and 'Dear Lord Jesus . . .' (p 59) from *Prayers for Children* by Meriel Rhodes; The Clarendon Press for the Sikh prayers (pp 20 and 29) from *The Sikh Religion* by Macauliffe; The Community of St Andrew for prayers on pages 8, 16, 19, 20 and 56; Curtis Brown Ltd and the Estate of Ogden Nash for 'Now another day is breaking . . .' (p 40) by Ogden Nash from *Parents Keep Out*; Victor Gollancz for the lines of Albert Schweitzer from *God of a Hundred Names* by Barbara Greene and Victor Gollancz; David Higham Associates for 'A Prayer for Little Things' by Eleanor Farjeon from *Silver Sand and Snow* (Michael Joseph); Hodder and Stoughton Ltd for the prayer by Jamie Wallace from *A Month of Sundays*; The Lutheran World Federation for prayers by Margareta Melin, Leonard H Deneinge, Elsa Gonzalez Lasalle, Fanny Camara-Macauley, Elizete Simon and Barn och bön; Macmillan Publishers Ltd for 'The Prayer of the Little Ducks' and 'The Prayer of the Tortoise' by Carmen Bernos de Gasztold from *Prayers from the Ark*; The National Christian Education Council for 'Dear Jesus . . .' (p 12) by Anne Farncombe from *Dear Father God* and 'Thank you, Father God' (p 14) and 'Father God' (p 17) by Mary Bacon and Jean Hodgson from *Prayers to use with Under Fives*; The National Spiritual Assembly of the Bahá'ís of the United States and the Bahá'í Publishing Trust for the prayers by Abdu'l-Bahá (p 72) from *Bahá'í Prayers and Tablets for the Young*; Peters, Fraser and Dunlop Ltd for lines by Hilaire Belloc; James Roose-Evans for 'Night-time' © 1988 James Roose-Evans; The Scripture Union for 'For our Pets' by Zinnia Bryan from *Let's Talk to God*; Professor Harmindah Singh for his prayer (p 78); The Society for Promoting Christian Knowledge for the prayer by Amy Carmichael from *Edges of his Ways*.

Every effort has been made to trace the copyright holders but the Publisher apologises if any inadvertent omission has been made.